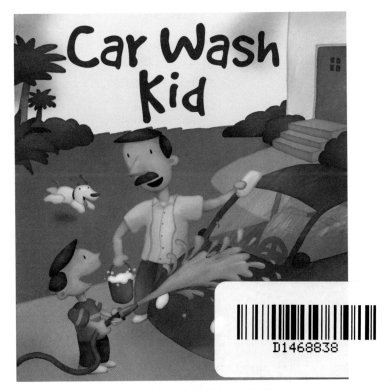

Written by Cathy Goldberg Fishman
Illustrated by Barry Gott

SCHOLASTIC INC.

New York Toronto London Auckland Sydney
Mexico City New Delhi Hong Kong Buenos Aires

With love to Xan and Matthew, my favorite car wash kids
—C.G.F.

For Finn
—B.G.

Reading Consultants

Linda Cornwell
Literacy Specialist

Katharine A. Kane
Education Consultant
(Retired, San Diego County Office of Education
and San Diego State University)

ISBN 0-516-24471-X

12 11 10 9 8 7 6 5 4 3 2 1   3 4 5 6 7 8/0

Printed in the U.S.A.   61

First Scholastic paperback printing, September 2003

A dirty car.
Look and see.

Car wash time
for Dad and me.

Dad is Soap Man.

Get that dirt!

Dad puts soap on.

Then I squirt.

We rub hard.

Soap suds fly.

Soap Man helps me reach up high.

The car is clean!
See what we did?

Now Dad calls me
Car Wash Kid.

Word List (38 words)

a	for	me	that
and	get	now	the
calls	hard	on	then
car	helps	puts	time
clean	high	reach	up
Dad	I	rub	wash
did	is	see	we
dirt	kid	soap	what
dirty	look	squirt	
fly	man	suds	

About the Author

Cathy Goldberg Fishman lives in Augusta, Georgia, with her husband, Steven, and two children, Alexander and Brittany. She grew up in Atlanta and graduated from Lesley College in Cambridge, Massachusetts. She has been a teacher, day care director, and owner and operator of a children's bookstore. She now writes children's books. She has also written **Soup** in the **A Rookie Reader®** series.

About the Illustrator

Barry Gott lives in Cleveland, Ohio, where he draws, sleeps, draws, eats, draws, plays with his son, draws, checks the mail, and draws some more.